PIANO DELLA CITTA DI MILANO E SVO CASTELLO

Milan in an XVIII century plan.

RENZO CHIARELLI

GET TO KNOW
MILAN

Translated by
SUSAN GLASSPOOL

BONECHI - EDITORE - FLORENCE

5, Via dei Rustici

Giovanni Migliara (1785-1837) - *The Piazza of the Duomo in Milan*

2

GET TO KNOW MILAN

Can one know a city like Milan deeply? Perhaps yes, perhaps no, it depends: one can try, however, to understand it, as we attempt to do in a few pages, looking it its exterior forms above all, but also trying to penetrate its « inside », across and over the curtain walls. It is clear that we are not proposing to make an analysis here, neither thorough, nor complete — as very many others have already made, and splendidly — of Milan, its culture, costume, life and productive capacity: we attempt much more simply to give a succinct representation in an equally short visual synthesis, conducted through « appointed places » across a selected sequence of flashes.

However, Milan, to begin with, is a city that one must study carefully, even from the outside. A city of difficult topography, where the antique reticle of the Romans has been cancelled and overwhelmed by the intricate disorder of the mediaeval streets and by all that has come after: disembowelments, vertical, horizontal, diagonal and radial cuts, especially in the whole of the last century, so that the city is ramified and spread out as God and many development plans, (from the one in 1865 to the prosopopeiae ones of the Lictorian age), have willed. The canals covered over, the Spanish bastions cast down, for a long time already it has been lost in the most part, — and even if that is not everything — that which in the epoch of Stendhal figured among the most beautiful cities in Europe. Perhaps no other Italian city is openly revealed like Milan over the urbanistic stratifications, in its metamorphasis and continued growth. The passage from old to not so old, to the new, comes in fact here in the middle of operations « in sight », like pieces of mosaic which fit into place one after another; in this way it shifts from antique to modern, from liberty to the pretentious « twentieth century », to functional and futuristic architecture of today: all of it, maybe, assembled in the same way. In this, Milan is a city full of contradictions: the skyscrapers and, in a step, the old and blackened houses which the contrast makes humbler and more dismaying. It happens therefore, that the palaces of a, however, declared architectural value (and there are many), often appear placed in an unrelated setting and in an indifferent connective: and even more so are the city gates, (some are very beautiful, like the Postern of St. Ambrose or the turreted Porta Ticinese or the Porta Nuova, which one cannot look at without Barbarossa coming to mind every time), cut off from their natural context by the destroyed walls, and not less than others later, they figure like the mythical testimony of worlds replaced one after the other, but lost just the same.

It is said that, luckily, all of monumental Milan (meaning also the « minor » things), and romantic Milan, dear to Stendhal and to Porta, to Grossi, and even now, to De Marchi, consacrated in the views of Inganni and Migliara, is definately not lost. That Milan still remains in the ambiguous and contorted movement of the many old streets, in the aristocratic and detached severity of others wich are more solemn: one for example, is Via Brera, or there are other very beautiful ones between Via Manzoni and Montenapoleone, (this latter is the most « Parisian » of the Milanese roads, because of its singular assonance of form, volume and quality), and of the « hawsers » of the peripheric Canals. This «-secret soul » of the old Milan remains in the rare surviving stone covered pavements, in the houses « with the galleries with the stench of cats, and with the flowering vases of March » which Buzzi recounts, in the underneath part of the porticoes which lead to the interior of the low courtyards by long terraces with the bannisters of iron or wood, in the funeral drapes which decorate a doorway if a misfortune has occured inside, in the pathetic note of the colour which springs out sometimes from the pink slabs of the many paviments and even pinker if it rains.

« It is necessary to wind up — wrote Piovene in his by now classic « Voyage in Italy » — the com-

3

mon thought that this region (Lombardy) and this city Milan is inferior in beauty to the rest of Italy ». It is right: it is also necessary to add, beyond another easily, for us, contestible common thought, however accredited between the public less prepared and the tourists, hurried and conditioned by the routine of the travel agencies: which is that Milan is not a « city of art », even if in effect it is the city which escapes, to again repeat Piovene, « the sealed beauty of other Italian cities, which are often limited, a prison· for those who live in them; with a final perfection which sometimes condemns them to sterility ». Instead one could say that Milan is full of art and artistic· phenomenons; neither do we intend to say by that, only those officially proclaimed or sanctioned by notoriety (Galleries and Museums like the Brera, the Castello Sforzesco, the Ambrosian, the Poldi-Pezzoli, or very famous monuments like the Duomo, St. Ambrogio or the Grazie would be enough in this case); but also, and moreover, artistic facts are scattered all over the city, and often require, it is a question of conspicuous works also, the fatigue of research; but which most times they then concede the recompense of the surprise. From the Roman and protochristian vestiges, and in fact from the monuments of the Romanesque and Gothic Middle ages and the Renaissance — with the great insertions by Leonardo and Bramante — to a sumptuous baroque, to an eighteenth century illuminated by Tiepolo, to the neoclassicism of Cagnola, Piermarini and Appiani, to the romanticism of Hayez and Induno, to mention only a few names, until, the futurism of Boccioni, the history of Milanese art is projected within a very accomplished and grandiose arch, and is so much greater when it sparkles with real light as in the epoch of the Visconti and the Sforza: then it deals with Jacopino da Tradate or Giovannino de' Grassi, Michelino da Besozzo or Bembo, Matteo Raverti or Amedeo, Butinone or Zenale, Bergognone or Foppa. Neither, on the other hand, can one forget that even today, with Rome, Milan is the major Italian centre of artistic production.

This goes for the culture generally, for which Milan, a city endowed with a good three Universities and by illustrious Libraries, the essential point of Italian editorials and journalism, primary centre of Institutes of European importance, unmistakably has tied the real name to all Italian culture from its origins until today (and this is said, however, only of the humanistic culture, and only rising to mention in its position in the field of scientific research), with very high points in the eighteenth and nineteenth centuries, from Giuseppe Pariti to the « licentious » (making only one name in the middle, that of Alessandro Manzoni). The same is said for music, for which Milan, in the nineteenth and early twentieth centuries was the unquestioned capital, thanks above all to La Scala and the Casa Ricordi (useless to say that Verdi, not Milanese, fused himself together with Milan, and remains so in the universal memory). Finally, if there is a place where the theatre really and profoundly lives still, that is Milan: Milan which, faithful to the most remote and glorious of her traditions, has known how to create today, among other things, an instrument of undoubtable perfection, which is its, « Little Theatre ».

It is not possible to make the portrait of a city like Milan in a few lines. One will finish however by pointing out, even at the cost of repetition, a fact which stays with us in our hearts and which, felt more or less confusedly by many Italians, is however warned and meant by very many poets: which, namely Milan, in spite of its dynamism and its positive rationality, is still today the Italian city in which the pleasant shadows of an almost nostalgic romanticism delay most (perhaps more European than Italian, and however, very different from those of Venice or Naples), and of a peculiar conservatism, which when it can, is shown in the most divers ways: in the lyric season at La Scala like the yellow risotto with saffron (in no other place has a domestic plate reached, we believe, such a high emblematic value) or in the big Milanese cakes, in the uncalmed memory of the Canal which is no more, or in the mourning for the lost « carriage drivers », in the surviving tracks of the trams, in the pride of the « oh, beautiful! » in Piazza Sant'Ambrogio, in the kind florist fin du siècle, under the shining and pretentious porticoes of Piazza Meda, in the old signs painted by hand which remain a little everywhere. An undecipherable and subtle, but persevering sentiment, which has not been entirely overwhelmed by the evolution of time, but which lives together with it, although remaining isolated perhaps protected by the dome of fog which hinders all of its vanishing; a state of mind with the impenetrable appearance, but in whose depth, if one keeps one ears open, one can sometimes hear the easy prose of Emilio De Marchi run over or plaintive but clear, the triumphal and candidly progressionist notes of the « Excelsior Ball » resound. The Madonnina, herself, luminous and golden, held in the middle between earth and sky in the darkness of the Milanese nights, is a distant apparition, mirage and warning, and is not only an apex of civic pride and piety: it is also, and above all, a more than human concentration of tenderness and poetry. The poetry, modest and subdued, of Milan.

The Basin of the Porta Ticinese,
in an etching
by A. Carbonati in 1926.

THE HISTORY OF MILAN

There is no other Italian city, excluding Rome, that re-assumes so much a part of the history of Italy in itself, and which, at a certain point, rather, becomes Italy itself. Firstly then, it was the Roman *Mediolanum*, capital in the third century of the already declining Empire of the West, then, from the V to the VIII came the invasions of the Visigoths, Huns and Ostrogoths, and therefore the decadence; but in the IV century, a luminous and splendid page was written by the great Bishop Ambrose, later Saint and protector of the city. Yet more figures of Bishops, Princes and warriors in the dawn of the Middle Ages, between the IX and XI centuries: Angilberto II, Ansperto di Biassonio and, the greatest of all, Ariberto d'Antimiano, who determined the political structure which gave life to the free Council. The age of the Council was that of iron and blood and yet it was glorious, signed above all by the battles against the Emperor of Germany, Federico Barbarossa, when Milan won and lost, was destroyed and rose again finally to redeem the real freedom in the battle of Legnano in March 1176.

In the internal battles between the Torriani and the Visconti, the latter came out victorious, and from 1311 to 1450 remained uncontested lords of the city. For half a century the Seigniory of the Sforza followed and it is really during the Visconti-Sforza period that Milan reached its greatest political, economic and artistic splendour. Three and a half centuries of almost uninterrupted foreign domination followed: French, Spanish (and here two singular figures of Bishops shine, Carlo and Federico Borromeo, the cardinal in the *Promessi Sposi*), and longest of all, the Austrians. A brief interval — in the Napoleonic period, from 1797 to 1814 — during which Milan was capital successively of the Cisalpine Republic, the Italian Republic and the Kings of Italy. Then again, Austrian domination, which, however, this time had to do with the growing insufference of the Italian liberals, particularly the Milanese: there were episodes culminating in the famous « Five days » of March 1848. In the centre of the first two Italian wars of independence, Milan was liberated in 1859 and perhaps, from then onwards, started to be the « moral capital » of Italy. Destined to be at the bottom of the most grandiose national events, even in the last fifty years, (Fascism was born and died in Milan), the city, heart of the Italian Resistance, and however very hardly tried by the bombing, suffering and reprisals, really watched the end of the War on the front of Southern Europe in its squares in April 1945.

THE DUOMO

There is little to do: in Italy when one says « the Duomo », one immediately thinks, by instinct, who knows why, of the Duomo in Milan: of the forest of spires, cusps, pinnacles, statues, of the patient and immense continuous work, of perforation, chisel work, and burin which seem to make its facade, its sides, its apse; to that spiritual vertex of Gothic that makes its interior. One can also call the other Italian « cathedrals » by name: Santa Maria del Fiore, San Marco, San Petronio; the Duomo of Milan, although it also has a name (it is dedicated in fact to *Maria Nascente*) instead: it is « the Duomo » and no more, the Duomo for antonomasia, *el Domm*.

Whoever has not yet seen the Duomo of Milan, it figures as all white from a distance when one imagines it: instead its colour is indefinable, between grey, golden yellow, brown, pale pink, and violet, depending on the direction of light. Fault of the fog and the « smog » which blacken and crack it, and of the varnish of time and other things; but one understands the secret of the « changing » colour of the Duomo by looking well from close to, and it is in the quality of the same marble used in the covering, the marble of Candoglia, by its own nature (let us transcribe from a learned authorative Guide, that of the Italian Touring Club), « rosy white, lightly pearled with incarnate shade and bluish veining ».

In truth one cannot say that the Piazza of the Duomo — architectural speaking — is a marvel: neither for unity and coherence of style (on the contrary, there are many styles) nor for authority and beauty of form; and neither is it a square that is represented for its « picturesqueness », as many are in Italy. However, other than majestic, it is a « terribly sympathetic » square, and God knows why! For its vitality, for its incessant and joyous movement, for the people and the windows under the porticoes: perhaps for a certain literary position that there is

underneath, or maybe because, simply, it is the Piazza of the Duomo of Milan. Then there is, exactly, the Duomo: a monument that can and cannot give pleasure (especially to excessive « classicists »); but also a monument that undoubtedly surprises, conquests, fascinates and with such a personality of itself alone, to make all the rest seem lost. The least beautiful parts of the square are really the houses on the opposite side to the Duomo: with insignificant, clumsy facades; but is really from there with the fall of darkness, that the evening bursts and the miracle is kindled. The blaze of multi-coloured lights, glittering, rotating and flying that is alternated, superimposed, and succeeded with incessant and disconcerting rythm, difficult to follow (*instead of stars* — wrote Umberto Saba — *words light up every evening*). Well then, even the square can become marvellous.

> *Duomo of Milan*
> *Frozen*
> *Buried overthrow*
> *Here is the natural cathedral*
> *Of the caves of Postumia*
>
> (Farfa)

Who made the Duomo of Milan? The reply is difficult, if not, impossible, really: from the moment that the Duomo of Milan is one of those grandiose collective works formed across the centuries, in the way of a slow geological stratification, and around which an undeterminable number of men have worked along an uninterrupted series of generations like, (pardon the abusive simily) busy ants. The first reason for the construction of the Duomo was the unexpected fall of the belfry of the « winter basilica » of Santa Maria Maggiore, on April 11th 1353 which dramatically showed the necessity of a new cathedral. The problem was made concrete

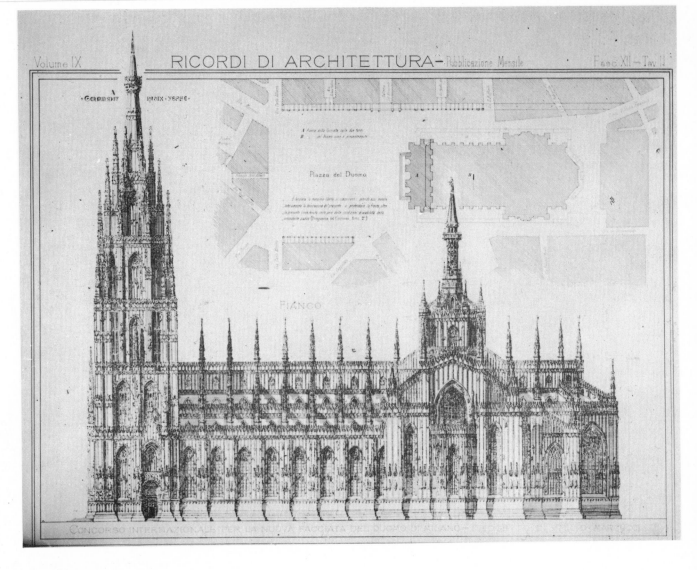

towards the end of the century, at the start of that authentic « Renaissance » manifested in Milan during the government of the « Count of Virtue », Gian Galeazzo Visconti, who rose to power in 1385.

Historians indicate that with every probability in 1385-86 the start of the ponderous construction was determined not only by the willingness of the prince, but also by the shared enthusiasm of all the people, and under the authorative stimulus of the Archbishop Antonio da Saluzzo, a plan was adopted anyhow to look for and provide the indispensible financial means towards the gigantic enterprise. The same project of the building, was also, almost certainly collective, and it was superintended, beginning to end, by Italian and foreign masters, giving place to one of the most colossal « equipes » of history.

The Works for building were started, as was the custom, in the east, and therefore with the apse; and proceeded by sweeping away, little by little, the old construction that encumbered the ground.

It is not our job in this article and in very reduced space to recall all the very long history of a construction carried on for about five centuries, (« long like the construction », the Milanese still say), and which has only been finished for a short time: only some facts consequently and the most important names. The first of these is that of Simone da Orsenigo, master builder of the construction until 1391 (it rests confined to the limits of fantasy, the hypothesis of a unitary project owed to Andrea da Modena, or outright to the same Gian Galeazzo), who was succeeded by a real superabundance of masters,

among whom were Marco and Bonino da Campione, Nicholas de Bonaventure, Giovanni da Friburgo, Ulrico da Fussingen, Giovanni Mignot, and many others: a prominent role revolves around, until the year of his death in 1398, Giovanni de' Grassi, painter, sculptor, miniaturist, and architect, a « just man and loyal friend of the Construction », at the time when the interior pilasters were being raised and they were starting to throw out the vaults. When Gian Galeazzo Visconti died in 1402 the interference by foreign masters ceased contemporarily; meanwhile, the wonderful boring of the great windows over the apse was created and they started to join together the glass for the windows; in 1418 Pope Martino V consecrated the main altar. From 1414 to 1448, Filippino degli Organi was director of work,

and was followed, under Francesco Sforza, by Giovanni and Guiniforte Solari: in the meantime the tiburium was raised, the dome of which would have been finished by Amadeo and Dolcebono in the September of 1500. Here a pause: the work was started in 1547; from '67 to '85 the masterbuilder was Pellegrino Pelligrini, who induced some particulars of the interior in a baroque style, in the spirit of the Counter-reformation (it was not for nothing Pellegrini was the man of trust of San Carlo Borromeo); this same Pellegrini also proposed two different solutions for the facade and had at his side, at some point, Galeazzo Alessi, the projector of the underground chapel called the « scurolo ». There was serious thought about the facade, only from 1590 however, firstly with Martino Bassi, then with Lelio

Buzzi and Francesco Maria Richini to whom — protected by Cardinal Federico Borromeo — fell the honour of setting it out in 1631, keeping for the present, in the lower part, the designs of Pellegrini. The work of Richini was continued by the architect Carlo Buzzi, notwithstanding strong criticisms moved against him by the great Gian Lorenzo Bernini. Meanwhile all the covering of the building was completed, and the interior was overpopulated with baroque sculpture; work on the facade was closed with the death of Buzzi in 1658; there was a great deal of talking done for a century and half, but without much conclusion: instead a better sort of result was the conclusion of the central spire of the tiburium, finished by Francesco Croce between 1765 and '69: then in 1774, the golden statue of the « Madonnina », glory and symbol of Milan, was triumphantly arranged upon it. To definately push the enterprise, the expedious and stubborn willingness of Napoleon was needed, who crowned Emperor in the Duomo in 1805, ordered it to be finished as quickly as possible with the facade: the same facade was, in fact, completed finally in 1809 from a design by Carlo Amati. But the work continued for a good while: it was only in 1906 that the main doorway was completed by Pogliaghi's bronze shutters; while the competition for the last of the doors, that on the right, was very near to us in time (1952-53).

The phantasmagoric confusion of spires, big spires, pinnacles, cusps, buttresses, rampant arches, cyma, acroteria, perforations, and ornate style, which of these makes the Duomo seem as though it is covered by the most hallucinating, petrified vegetation that one has ever seen? one can find it hard to believe, but the largest part of it was decorated in the nineteenth century, the work of those « enterprising cultivators » (as recently Mia Cinotti well defined) who were the various Amati, Pestagalli, Vandoni, Cesabianchi; but the seed is far from the spirit of late Gothic that had animated Italian, German and French artists towards the end of the fourteenth and early fifteenth centuries, and to whom, although in a deviation of taste and in a deformity of interpretation, every generation of artifices remained — generally — faithful, in the long climb across the centuries: also where the vision was frozen in little less than a mechanic repetition of forms, next anyway to the cultural schemes of the *Gothic-revival*. But the same destiny touched many even the great Gothic monuments of Oltralpe, growing over the centuries: to start with one of the most august of them, the Duomo of Colonia.

We will not speak here of the precious treasures that the Duomo of Milan has collected, (paintings, statues, tomb monuments, goldsmithery, tapestries, materials, marquetry and marbles); neither of the stupifying plastic incrustations which recover the sides and is clinging to the pinnacles, linked also to an innumerable series of names of marble workers and sculptors of every land; nor of the stupendous stained glass windows, renewed in everlasting sequence, (many of them were shattered after the joyous salute of the artillary saluting Napoleon as crowned Emperor, also): neither of the unlimited variety of views which contemplation of the great construction offers from every angle: from low down, from above, along the colossal sides, of the sudden appearence at the end of the immense apse and above it, of the inexhaustible, and very subtle play of the decorations and the perforations.

The interior of the Duomo of Milan. Five grandiose naves, very high, divided by powerful fascias of pilasters, carrying the ogive arches and from which diverge the daring frames of the crossbeams; between the pilasters and arches is the lofty pause of the tabernacle style capitals, these designed by Giovanni de' Grassi, and similar to flowery knots of Gothic ivory Bishop's staves. The transept and the deambulatory for the use of France in the apse. Spirituality subjugating, mystic giddiness and suggestions of the sublime: words and phrases recurring on the hundred vaults in a very copious literature; neither is there any value in repeating them. Ojetti, displaying an inimmune critiscism, perhaps to some classicist defect, believed he saw in the Duomo of Milan, the triumph of the « squared Latin conscience that resists for the whole of the fourteenth century to the floods of Gothic whims, etc. ». It may be so, but to us, admiring the interior of this church, born at the geographical margins of « true » Gothic, and although in the epoch of a Gothic in its decline, seems instead to breathe sometimes a Gothic so much more « Gothic » that one could not breathe much more of it in one of the cathedrals of Oltralpe.

Dedicated to lovers of figures and precise notes. The Duomo of Milan is the largest of all the Gothic churches and is the second, absolutely, in the world after St. Peter's in Rome, (length 158 metres, breadth 93 metres, height, to the head of the Madonnina, 108 metres). There are 135 spires, decorated with 1537 statues. On a clear day, from the « terraces » of the Duomo, one can enjoy the luminous view of the Alpine group dominated by Monte Rosa.

13

7. - SAN GOTTARDO

Of the ancient church of San Gottardo are left practically only the steeple and the apse: the steeple, visible from many points in the centre of Milan, seems placed on purpose there to make a way, in a sense, between the forest of spires of the Duomo and the squared up and aggressive mass of the Torre Velasca. It is the most beautiful steeple in Milan; its octagonal framework in brick, flings itself very elegantly towards the height, starting from a squared stone base; the delightful brick frames swaddle it in small interlacing Gothic arches, and very long stone pilasters, like endless tubes of drainpipes, which represent the corners in profile. An arcade of arches and little columns with crutch capitals, springs very nimbly out on the top landing and the motif is repeated with splendid effect in the belfry, which is of more subtle framework, surmounted by the conical cusp. The belfry was constructed by Francesco Pecorari, and the apse of the church soberly echoes the themes, lower down.

The Church of San Gottardo was erected in around 1336, at the order of Azzone Visconti, perhaps on a design by the same Pecorari. The interior, with only one nave with a vestibule, is no longer as it once was; it has become neoclassical; but, in compensation, it guards the fine funeral Monument of Azzone Visconti, the work of Giovanni di Balduccio, and it adorns itself with a fragment of the *Crucifixion* by the School of Giotto, attributed variously and previously situated outside, at the foot of the belfry.

8. - THE ARCADE

It was a great shame that Giuseppe Mengoni fell down from the top of a scaffolding placed in front of the eve of the inauguration: firstly because the Bolognese architect lost his life in the ruinous fall and secondly because he lost the opportunity, even for a short time, of feeling proud of the extraordinary success, which the Milanese decreed at once, of his creation of stone, cement, iron and glass, to which he had dedicated great meticulous care for twelve long and weary years, from 1865-1877. There is no other place in Milan, in fact which the Milanese feel and have always felt more « Milanese » than this Arcade, now just a century old; the ideal meeting place, of rest, of pleasant idling, and most adapted to make aquiantances and renew friendships, to contract business and discuss politics, art and literature; the « cosmopolitan » public, as one says, which is fatally attracted there during the « season », is obli-

ged to feel itself in there, also like the *Milanese*. The Arcade, a useful and easy walk between the Duomo and La Scala, the topographical and mondane epicentre of the city, entitles itself after Vittorio Emanuele 11 (the iconclastic toponymy at the end of the Second World War has left it immune and represents one of the most interesting Italian products of that awkward sympathetic taste (half European-futuristic, half provincial-representative) which in Italy generally goes by the name of « Umbertine style », and which in this case, luckily, has not created the irreparable waste caused instead in many other places; there concur the bold, for those times, metal structure of the vaults and of the great dome, the gilding, the stuccos, the questionable neo-

baroque and neorenaissance juncture, the pompous allegories in mosaic high up in the large lunettes. The Milanese have made this, their Arcade, the « drawing room » of the city, full of expensive shops, restaurants and cafes, in some of which are held meetings, for spaces of ten years, of the flowers of figurative art, of literature and of fine Italian singing.

Giuseppe Ungaretti, the poet has seen the Arcade like this:

An eye of stars
Which spys at us from that pool
And filters its frozen benediction
On this aquarium of sleepwalking boredom.

(G. Ungaretti, *In The Arcade*)

16

9. - THE THEATRE AT LA SCALA

One should say « Theatre at La Scala » (or more simply, « La Scala ») says Milan, says Verdi, Donizetti, Rossini, Bellini, Ponchielli, Puccini, Mascagni, Boito; says the Italian Renaissance, says Toscanini, says the most celebrated of the « First Nights », says the first and most illustrious lyric theatre of the world. There really is something there to leave oneself intimidated in thought alone as to how many musicians, librettists, conductors, tenors, bass, baritones, mezzosopranos, contraltos, ballerinas, choreographers and stage designers have tied the right name to La Scala in little less than two centuries, from when the Theatre was opened on August 3rd, 1778 with the *Recognised Europe* by Antonio Salieri from Legnago.

Where La Scala is now, constructed by Giuseppe Piermarini in 1776-78, there stood in ancient times (from this comes the name of the Theatre) the Church of Santa Maria della Scala, erected in 1381 by Beatrice della Scala, bride of Bernabò Visconti; the building, of precise and noble neoclassical form on the outside, boasts inside one of the most splendid and perfect eighteenth century halls, with four types of boxes and two galleries, exquisitely decorated. The Theatre Museum, the « Little Scala », the Stage Design Laboratory and the Dancing School, make part of the complexity of « La Scala »; in the « foyer », on the occasion of the « First Nights », the most elegant international public encircle that traditional place, the *tout - Milan*.

10. - THE COURTYARD OF PALAZZO MARINO

Galeazzo Alessi from Perugia (c. 1512-1572) was brought up in Rome, breathing the air of Michelangelo and Bramante, and absorbing by instinct and for study the rigorous themes together with pictorial architecture « copious with light », from Serlio. Although the activity of Alesso — and with it, his highest glories — stayed above all confined to Genoa and Liguria, where he unrolled « an original architectural language run through with a refined sense of colour » (Becherucci) and like many, very much admired by Rubens, the artist was often in Milan, and precisely, from 1553-1558 he carried out the Palace for the rich Genoese Tommaso Marino (or De Ma-

rini), Duca di Terranova. This Palace, left unfinished, was brought to a conclusion in 1888-90, by the architect Luca Beltrami and today houses the Milanese Council.

The highest part of architectural relief in this Palace is undoubtedly the *courtyard,* very ornate, where in the clear planning of the design, rich with Serlian influences, the ostentatious pictoricism of hermae, statues, large masks, trophies, plaques, niches and festoons are distended and accumulated: that which A. Venturi judged — perhaps with excessive severity — « false and encumbering ».

11. - SAN CARLO AL CORSO

He who is not used to such a type af surprise — which is anything but infrequent in Milan — would certainly not expect to meet by chance in a neoclassical church, (and what a large building!) with a relative square with porticoes right here, in this special sort of marble entrenchment which has become in recent times the Corso Vittorio Emanuele 11 (the old Corsià dei Servi, dear to engravers and painters of the nineteenth century, especially to the late Epigoni of the « view » painting, starting with Migliara).

An example, at least of neoclassical architecture, we must however create also ourselves, in this our succinct and flowing *look,* and hold count that in Milan, the neoclassical is aboundingly and very much egregiously represented and it seems to us that the Church of San Carlo is, of the Milanese neoclassical buildings, among the most meritorious to mention, especially for that aulic and declared reference, outside and in, to the most « classic » among the monuments of Roman antiquity (obviously the Pantheon). *Dedicatum S. Carolo - MDCCCLVII:* the architecture is by Carlo Amantis the dome « vaulted without armatures » as one reads in the guide, is a work of Felice Pizzagalli, (1844).

12. - CRISTOFORO MORETTI
(known from 1451 to '75 and 1485)

Madonna and Child. - (Panel)
Poldi-Pezzoli Museum

The central part of the altarpiece, previously in the Chapel of Sant'Aquilino near San Lorenzo in Milan, is mentioned by P. Allegranza and by Lanzi, and partly reconstructed by Longhi in 1928 by joining the two side pieces of the Saints Genesis and Lawrence, also from the Poldi-Pezzoli Museum: the panel is the only one signed by the elegant and sensible Cremonese artist and is datable as around 1460.

Cristoforo Moretti (« *Christoforus de Moretti de Cremona pictor* ») although not far from the role of a « *convinced and probably invariable follower of the late cosmopolitan Gothicism* » (Longhi) is, however among the most convincing of the late Gothic Lombard painters and, at the same time, most representative of the taste of an atmosphere still extraordinarily open to suggestions from a Michelino da Besozzo, of the Zavattari and from the close Veronese school.

13. - ANTONIO DEL POLLAIOLO
(1428-1498)

Profile of a woman. - (Panel)
Poldi-Pezzoli Museum

This enchanting, very musical and incisive *profile,* which shows the glorious Florentine « portrait painter » of the second half of the fifteenth century in a superb and quintessencial way, likewise is the « highlight » of the Milanese Poldi-Pezzoli Museum (one of the most accredited and conspicuous artistic institutions of the city. Variously attributed by critics to Domenico Veneziano, Verrocchio, even to Leonardo in his youth, and finally to Piero del Pollaiolo, by Cruttwell, A. Venturi, Longhi, Toesca, Sabatini and Ortolani; Ragghianti sees in this portrait and its relation in the Berlin Museum, « the style of Pollaiolo in his most individual character ». The painting is of a doubtful chronology; the lady depicted here, believed by some to be the wife of Giovanni de' Bardi, was recognised by Venturi as the same as that in the portrait of Berlin.

14. - SAN SATIRO

San Satiro, or, better still, Santa Maria above San Satiro: here is another surprise and, at the same time, another example of the survival of the antique in the midst of the encroaching new. It is one of those Milanese monuments that one needs to have a little patience to go and look for among the large and small streets of the centre of Milan. It is a church of very old and illustrious origins since it was founded in the IX century by the Archbishop Ansperto and consecrated in 1036 by d'Intimiano (he who is famous in the battle against the Emperor Corrado Il Salico). Little has been conserved of the original, visible only in the interior in the *Cappella della Pietà,* whose archaic forms however were enclosed

by Bramante in the very elegant little temple on a circular plan. It is rightly such an extraordinary addition, that which remains, to exercise the surest fascination on whosover looks in from the outside, in this use of clear and reasoned harmony of the proper minute forms, which greatly serve the support and the back of the main construction and the austere counterpoint of the Romanesque belfry of the IX - XI centuries, the oldest in Milan.

It was Bramante who took in hand the direction of work in around 1480, for the reconstruction of the ancient monument and who planned, in 1482, the successive extension that has been carried out, in definative, in the construction of a T-shape desi-

gned new church which amply echoes (inevitable for Bramante) the immortal forms of Brunelleschi, and where the most striking thing of all, is the daring of the false perspective on the walls, around the main altar, and the exquisite and very graceful *Baptistery,* also by Bramante, in an octagonal design and with two kinds of arcades (with a frieze and tondoes in terracotta by Agostino de Fonduti). The principal facade of the church is, instead cold, not to say glacial, started by Amedeo in 1486, but finished — in very correctly academic terms, however — by G. Vandoni in 1871.

15. - PIAZZA MERCANTI

It is a part of Renaissance and mediaeval Milan miraculously left intact in the great bustle which convulses the city in the process of modernisation; and it still gives a surprise to find oneself inside it, as in an embalmed abstract thing. It is also one of the places where colour can be perceived most, dominated almost everywhere else by the grey tones, (although noticing that the colour of Milan, even in this case — never proclaims itself in an over obvious or lively way). This square is, finally, a noble and splendid huddle of epochs and styles; one can identify there the mediaeval Forum of Milan, formed here round about when the Council was transferred, when it left the Broletto Vecchio in 1228. Originally it was a « closed » square, with six openings placed in correspondence to the equal number of quarters of the city.

Although between themselves the buildings of this square are very different, they harmonise singularly, giving the place — in virtue of an undiciferable *concordia discors* — a complex atmosphere which is extraordinarily unitary. Let us start with the most famous and antique building, the *Palazzo della Ragione,* or the *Broletto Nuovo,* which has a facade also onto the Via Mercanti: a rigorous and essential construction, sitting on triple lines of arcades which come up from a raised platform, decorated with bicoloured caps. In the upper part of the facade, in very simple brickwork, large tri-foil windows open off in Romanesque frames. The Palace was built between 1228 and 1233 by Mayor *Oldrado da Tresseno,* who is represented here on horseback in a bass relief of the style of Benedetto Antelami, of 1233. This bears the Latin inscription which exalts the many merits of the great magistrate (discussable among these, in todays taste, is that of having had the heretics burnt; but all the same, neither was the great St. Ambrose very tender in respect to these people, as we know). The beautiful proportions of the Palace were altered in 1770 by heightening it for the use of the Archivio Notarile. Things unfortunately of all times.

On the opposite side of the square, two other interesting buildings, placed side by side, naturally contrast; the first, and the oldest, (unfortunately legible only from the interpretation given by the restoration of 1904, which was intended to remedy the disfigurement of the seventeenth and eighteenth centuries), is the *Loggia degli Osii,* erected at the order of Matteo Visconti in 1316. This exhibits alternate Romanesque and Gothic forms in the portico, in the arcade and in the trifoils of the top floor (everything in the connective of an ornament of black and white marbles): a fascia of heraldic emblems (the shields of the quarters of the city and of the viscountcy) adorns the parapet of the arcade, in the centre of which, juts out the *assembly* or *speaker's balcony,* which served the heralds for making proclamations of edicts or sentences, and the Councillors and the Mayor for speaking to the people, (the use, in this sense, that our balconies have for us and is of very ancient roots!) The nearby palace, constructed in baroque style by Carlo Buzzi in 1645, is that of the *Scuole Palatine,* and has no particular merit, neither is it very original, in how it makes a repetition of the sixteenth century structure of the Palazzo dei Giureconsulti, in the nearby Via Mercanti, with a dearth of fantasy. The Scuole Palatine — in olden days « del Broletto » — was very important under the Visconti and the Sforza and also in the successive centuries: one remembers, by incidence that in the eighteenth century, Cesare Beccaria and Giuseppe Parini gave lessons here.

Completing the square in the north west, is *the Palazzo dei Notai* and what remains of the *Casa dei Panigarola:* a fifteenth century building of late Gothic style, with elegant frames and brickwork moulding. Neither can one miss the well of custom in such an atmosphere; and the well that is in fact a fine puteal of the XVI century, with regular eighteenth century additions in front of the Loggia degli Osii.

16. - THE BRERA PALACE

The Jesuits built their College in 1591, from a design by the architect Martino Bassi, in the place where the Convent degli Umiliati stood in ancient times. The building conceived in a grandiose form, was continued starting in 1615 by Francesco Maria Richini, who left his masterpiece in the ample and very much in proportion rectangular courtyard, characterised by the harmonious placing of the two kinds of gallery above with arcades supported by elegant twin columns: the two floors are linked by a great monumental staircase with a double flight of steps. In the centre of the courtyard, which keeps to the traditional cobbled pavimentation, softened by a light down of grass, rises up the bronze statue of Napoleon I, the work of Antonio Canova.

The Brera Palace holds cultural Institutions of very high sounding, like the *Braidense National Library*, the *Academy of Fine Art*, the *Lombard Institute of Science and Letters*, and the *Astronomical Observatory*; but the most illustrious presence in it is certainly that of the *Brera Pinacotheque*, which traces its origins from the foundation of the Academy of Fine Art in 1776, desired by the Empress Maria Teresa and very much increased by Napoleon himself, has today come to be one of the most conspicuous collections of painting in Italy and in Europe.

17. - RAFFAEL SANZIO (1416-1492)

Wedding of the Virgin. - (Panel) The Brera Pinacotheque.

Raffael signed and dated this famous work of his youth: on the entablature of the colonnade which surrounds the temple in the background of the scene (derived, it seems, from the little temple by Bramante of St. Peter in Montorio in Rome from 1502) one in fact reads the inscription: *Raphael Urbinas,* and, lower down, the date: MDIIII. The panel was painted for the Albizzini family and placed in the Church of San Francesco in Città di Castello: it has been in the Brera from 1806. Still tied to open suggestions from Perugino, the work is however among those which best qualify the youthful activity of Raffael. « *The happy insertion of the temple in the moonshaped space, the rigorous connections between the architecture and the people... finally the function explained by light in joining intimately together the single parts, declare the personal achievements by the twentyone year old artist* (E. Camesasca, *Raffaello,* 1962).

18. - PIERO DELLA FRANCESCA (1416-1492)

Madonna with Son, Angels, Saints, and with Federico da Montefeltro, Duca d'Urbino (Panel) Brera Pinacotheque

The « Urbino altarpiece », previously in the Church of San Bernardino of Urbino, and at the Brera from 1811, represents one of the most high and solemn moments in the art of Piero della Francesca: it is referable to around the years between 1470 and '75. « *This dominates before the oldest altarpieces, for its grandiose unity of conception. Piero in fact makes subtle use of the advantages in the noble relationship between the ten figures arranged in a semi-circle around the Virgin, and the architecture where the* *little pilasters and the mirrors made of porphyry and peacock blue, turning from the sides in foreshortening, in the hemicycle of the tribune, repeat around that sacred egg which descends from the shell from the semivault, the same composition of figures... The sollemn meeting is more than a sacred conversation then, preordinated and compuncted by the Bramantesque hall, before Bramante* ». (R. Longhi, *Piero della Francesca* 1927).

19. - BERNARDINO LUINI (known of from 1512-1531)

Madonna of the Rosary. - (Panel) Brera Pinacotheque

A « precious acquisition », for the Brera Pinacotheque, Corrado Ricci defined this panel as the main follower of Leonardo in Lombardy — Bernardino Luini to be exact. It was in the Certosa di Pavia a long time ago, and then passed into the hands of one Giuseppe Bianchi, and from there it came at last to the Brera Academy, for 12.000 lire, in 1825. It is a panel of dimensions too small to be an object of public cult, and instead it was probably destined for the cell of a friar: so A. Ottino Della Chiesa thinks, and he believes this painting by Luini is later than the frescoes in this same Certosa, and therefore datable as after 1525.

The very delicate work, of a luminous purity, is however to be found among the most convincing and affable paintings of the many carried out by the artist which this same Ottino Della Chiesa not unjustly defines as « the first humanistic lyric of the Lombard school of painting ».

20. - GENTILE BELLINI (1429-1507) and GIOVANNI BELLINI (1428-1516)

Detail of the *Sermon of Saint Mark in Alexandria*. - (Canvas) Brera Pinacotheque

The month of February in the year 1809 was passing: there was a great fervour of preparation in the gallery of the Brera Academy which was due to be inaugurated in some months from then, to be precise August 15th, the name-day of Napoleon. Canvases and panels arrived from all over the place, and on the 3rd February the great « teler » (m. 3,47x7,70) of the Sermon of St. Mark in the square of Alexandria which Gentile Bellini painted for the Great School of St. Mark in Venice and which was finished after his death by his brother Giovanni, arrived also in an enormous roll, together with other paintings.

The staged view painting *ante litteram* of Gentile found a way of expressing more free and grandiose terms in the large painting; his coloured fantasy was satisfied in creating fabulous surrealistic buildings and transforming the lyrical lagoon like atmosphere into a fabulous oriental landscape; his customary innate taste was exerted in the re-dressing of the rather strange fashions, oppressing the exoticism on the personages which people the scene. « *Note how easily the St. Mark's basilica is inserted in the scenery of the re-created Egyptian city, holding the eye* — notes G. A. Dell'Acqua — *the group of notable Venetians, and that taste of truth that it assumes in the talented stylistic transformation, and the swarms of beckoning women under the veils.*

SANT'AMBROGIO

Sant'Ambrogio of Milan: just « that old thing there, out of reach » by Giusti. Out of reach once, one understands: because now, instead, the Basilica of Sant'Ambrogio is practically in the centre of city (that which we are used to call, for some years now, the « historical centre »); and also the famous postern, which in olden days (to be precise, its two barrel-vaults faced entirely onto open country), fortified by two large towers designed to instil respect from a distance, has become a « piece of the museum », isolated and well catologued in Milan's heart.

The area in the centre from which rise up the most illustrious of the antique Milanese basilicas, is that which is thickest with memories and the glories of Imperial and Christian annals, if it is true that in it — as it seems — stood the Palace of Massimiliano, from whence Constantine would have promulgated the very famous *Edict* in 313, destined to give complete freedom to the Christian religion; next there was a palace of the German emperors in the X century; and there stands even now the *column of the devil,* where the devil in person, according to the legend, furiously battered his horns because of some bad disagreement with Saint Ambrose, (one can still clearly see the imprint). One understands, notwithstanding, how Francesco Petrarch came to live in such a place while he was in Milan.

It seems that Saint Ambrose founded by himself such a great monument, in the rest, he really merited it: Saint Ambrose, who in June of 387 had baptised no-one less than Saint Augustine: Saint Ambrose an energetic saint and persecutor of the Arians, but who did not hesitate to throw out the Emperor Teodosio from the Church because of his wickedness, and important to a point to become not only the patron saint, but completely the symbol of his Milan.

> .... *Saint Ambrose*
> *was a hieratic saint, enemy*
> *of idle disputes, censor of power*
> *of real things, incomprehensible*
> *for the soul much too tender ....*
>
> (C. Betocchi, *Squille di Lombardia*).

It was the same St. Ambrose, as they used to say, who had this basilica built in 379-387 which, in his progressive transformation had to finish as the masterpiece of Romanic architecture in Lombardy, and one of the greatest monuments of the Romanic period, *tout-court*. The most antique Ambrosian basilica was formed in the place previously occupied by the Christian cemetary *ad Martyres,* and was a church with three naves and a monoapse: inside, on April 5th 397, was celebrated St. Ambrose's solemn fulfillment, he was buried there next to the glorious remains of the martyred Saint Gervase and Protasio. At the side of the church, four centuries later, in 789, the Benedictine monks constructed their monastery; in the IX century the transformation of the church itself was started (the apse was lengthened, the steeple was raised higher, that which was called « of the monks »): between 1098 and 1128 the naves were reconstructed and a little later the Council had the second steeple erected (that « of the canons »), square, high and massive, in 1150, a new atrium, or *quadriportico,* replaced the previous ones of the epoch of the Archbishop Ansperto. From this moment the church already has the look which has been preserved in it over centuries, despite the ruins, the disfigurements and the baroque additions, the refacing, the restorations and the bombardments; and it was always to this famous basilica that the Emperors of the Sacred Roman Empire were conducted, to be crowned within: and where were buried at least four Kings (Pipino, Bernardo, Ludovico, Lotario), with the saints and martyrs. At the end of the fifteenth century Bramante intervened in the cloisters and in the presbytery; the ancient monastery which at least twice, had entertained among others, Barbarossa, today houses the Catholic University del Sacro Cuore.

One does not see very much from the outside: the tiburium rises up from above the compact lines of the burnt red coloured brick walls, the high part of the facade is, naturally, the two steeples of different size and height, which must singularise their traditional name to the differenciated use which they make on the inside, for the officiation, the monks and canons (on the right the first ones, on the left the second). The real suggestion starts as soon as one sets foot in the atrium, a very rare example among the survivors of a quadriportico: here the « catechumen » stood humbly, during the celebration of rites. In the severe space the solemn and bare facade is wonderfully arranged,

with two span roofs whose rythm corresponds well with the double ascent of the great arched opening of the arcade; an irregular « dowelling » of white marble scattered everywhere — in the arches resting on the ancient capitals, in their crowning in the form of small arches, in the ornament of the larger steeple — confers a precious picturesqueness to this famous « exterior ». All around under the portico are collected inscriptions, tomb seals, sarcophagi, bass reliefs: much of the late Romanic and high mediaeval history of Milan.

The severe majesty of the interior certainly does not let ones expectations down: few other churches know how to show with equal genuinity of language — in the massive force of the structure, in the refusal of every trimming, in the clever correspondence of the architectural elements — the intense and rarified spirituality of the primative centuries. Three naves, divided by a vigorous fascia of pilasters, the tight structure of the vaults and the jointures, the logical and bunched together sequence of the « matronea »: a sentiment of primordial and confident Christianity, aware of an esoteric and pregnant presence. A high tiburium hangs over the presbytery coherently finished by the three apses.

One would not speak separately of the many works of art which embellish Sant'Ambrogio: only of those which confirm the Romanic and Christian essence of the Basilica. First among these is the *Pulpit,* which, broken up in 1196 by the collapse of the vaults above, was reconstructed in 1201, keeping to the ancient form, the subtle and mysterious plastic decoration in the arches, in the frames, in the walls and continuing to collect the great Christian sarcophogi of the IV century, crowded with bass relief images, in its shade. In the centre of the presbytery, the *ciborium,* whose oldest parts are of the IX century, and which, lifted up on columns of porphyry, illustrates the glory of Christ and St. Ambrose in the gorgeous polycrome stuccoes on the four sides: under the canopy is the famous *Altar of Gold* (or altar front) of the IX century, the masterpiece of jewelled goldsmithery by the Master, Vuolvinio, and the very precious gift from the Archbishop Angilberto II. In the crypt an urn of crystal and gold contains the bones of the great Milanese saint, and of whom it is possible to admire from close up the very ancient portrait in mosaic decoration (V century) of the extremely old *Chapel of St. Victor in a Golden Sky.*

24. - THE HOUSE OF THE OMENONI

In few cases is the result of a contrast between old and new so pitiless and crude as between the moving and emotive facade of the *House of the Omenoni* (Via degli Omenoni) and the smooth and cold buildings built at its sides: it seems as though it has been saved out of mercy and once more the question comes spontaniously as to what must have been the aspect (and beauty) of Milan before.

The « omenoni », are the eight huge telamones which carry, or appear to carry, the architraves and portals of the picturesque little baroque facade of this house which Leone Leoni of Arezzo, « bizarre

spirit », constructed for himself towards 1573, enlivened with the mannerist « anti-renaissance » rule; the inner courtyard of porticoes is not disjointed from Tuscan reminders, in an analogous concept.

In this house Leoni, who was the « Caesarean sculptor » to Carlo V, was able to put together a discreet collection of antique works of art and those of his contemporaries; here he received his most important visitors: Giorgio Vasari, his fellow citizen was not the only one of these.

The eight vigorous and dramatic « omenoni » are works of the Lombard sculptor, Antonio Abbondio (1538-1591).

25. - PIAZZA CORDUSIO

Piazza Cordusio is, as one it wont to say, the « heart » of the varied circulation and a little also, of the Milanese topography. Here tram, bus, and underground flow together; a long and glittering underground footpath, of recent construction, unites « the Cordusio » with the sacred ground in front of the Duomo. Some of the most competent and famous arteries of the Milanese centre depart from the Cordusio also (Via Tommaso Grossi, Via Mercanti, Via Orefici, Via Broletto), and in the northwest, at the oval of the square, gush out from the funnel which is made, Via Meravigli and Via Dante (the latter is the most scenographical and « perspective » of the Milanese roads, with an authorative ending with the Castello and the Torre del Filarete). The ancient *curtis ducis* (the court of the Duke of Longobard was in fact here) is still in the place most solemnly representative of that pompous and vaguely « mitteleuròpeo » style of architecture, which characterised the Milan of the late ninteenth and early twentieth centuries; and the symbols of the might of the banking, commercial and insurance of Milan are concentrated there.

26. - MICHELANGELO MERISI DA CARAVAGGIO (1573-1616)

Basket of Fruit. - (Canvas) Ambrosian Pinacotheque.

The Ambrosian Pinacotheque makes an integral part of the great cultural mass which is exhibited in the Palace erected by Lelio Buzzi in 1603-09 at the wish of Cardinal Federico Borromeo (Manzoni speaks diffusely of this in the « Promessi Sposi »), to hold the famous Library and later an Academy of Fine Art, to which the Pinacotheque was annexed, precisely. If the Library can boast as among its most famous works, the *Virgil* of Petrarch, illuminated by Simone Martini and the *Boccaccio* of Venice from 1471, then the presence of the very famous *Atlantic Codes* of Leonardo, give unestimable lustre to the Pinacotheque.

The *Basket of Fruit* by Caravaggio is precisely, one of the paintings given to Ambrosian Library in 1618 by Cardinal Federico himself who described it in his « Museum » (*Nec abest gloria proximae huic fiscellae, ex qua flores micant. Fecit eum Michael Angelus Caravagiensis, ecc.* »).

« A basket of fruit against a yellow background, nothing more banal; but certain contours of the leaves, which are accentuated to suggest the light, bring the banal motif to the level of a masterpiece ». (L. Venturi, *Caravaggio,* 1951).

THE CASTELLO SFORZESCO

27. - THE MOAT AND THE TOWERS.
28. - THE DRAWBRIDGE

« *The standards of the Sforza / don't you see them wave? / Quickly into the saddle, my sturdy ones / the hour has come to fight!* ». I feel the old tale of Fusinato sounding in my ears, I do not know why, whenever I get to passing under the great gate of the Castello Sforzesco, surmounted by marmoreal reminders of the « good king » (Umberto I) who was assinated at Monza on July 29th 1900, and even higher up, by the statue of St. Ambrose.

The Castello Sforzesco is the most important chapter of civil Milanese architecture, and it is great luck that it has remained up until our times, because every moment in its long and troubled history, it ran the risk of being destroyed and swept away. The castle, truthfully, has not been called « of the Sforza » for long, its origins are, in fact, decidedly Visconti, and its history began when Galeazzo II Visconti had a *castrum* built in 1368 close by the Porta Giovia; later, between 1392 and 1396, Gian Galeazzo Visconti developed the original idea, raising a new and mòre ample building next to the same *castrum* (the « Citadel »). The luck of the castle was awarded when Filippo Maria Visconti stabilised his residence in it in 1412, and who was very much occupied with his manor house, reinforcing the structure and making it worthy of entertaining a prince's Court. At the death of Filippo Maria in 1447, the treachery of one certain Boilo, favourer of the Aragons, consigned the castle to the « Gilded Ambrosian Republic »; this, without many compliments, put the manor house to iron and fire, and destroyed it. When Filippo Maria's son-in-law, Francesco Sforza took possession of Milan, the obligation was not to reconstruct the castle; but in reality, in 1450 Sforza gave the commission to Giovanni da Milano and other architects, to put it all back together on its feet. They were joined by Jacopo da Cortina and in 1452, the Florentine Antonio di Pietro Averulino, nicknamed the Filarete, who designed the high middle tower of the main front. They proceeded on the work of extending and embellishing the castle without break, especially after 1466 when it became, under Galeazzo Maria, the stable residence of the Sforza, to whose tormented vicissitudes, from here onwards it was to be closely tied. Under Galeazzo Maria (killed in 1476) and during the regency of Bona di Savoia, famous artists like Bonifacio Bembo, Costantino da Varello, Giacomino Vismara and others co-operated in the decoration of the superb rooms; the tower, nicknamed « of Bona » was constructed from the design by the Marquis of Mantoa, Ludovico Gonzaga; new works arose in the Rocchetta and the Ducal Court. The ambitious and despotic Ludovico il Moro, lord of Milan from 1480,

called Leonardo da Vinci outright to him and entrusted him moreover with the erection of a great equestrian monument to Francesco Sforza: a monument which, lacking his translation into bronze, remained in terracotta and ended by being destroyed by the French in 1501.

The seat of one of the most brilliant and Maecenasesque Italian Courts remained only for a short time, moreover the castle very quickly joined obscure times: blockades and occupations on the part of the French, the Sforza and the Spanish were continued uninterruptedly in the space of a few decennea, and the royal palace transformed itself into a fortress. The decadence continued until the arrival of Napoleon (1796) who firstly saved the castle from the fury of the Jacobins; then in 1800 decreed its demolition, avoided by a hair's breadth thanks to the architect Antolini who talentedly inserted the Visconti-Sforzesque block into the project of the Bonaparte Forum: only the ramparts and the Spanish bastions fell. Another great risk was in 1884, this time on account of the regulator plan, and a new generous help was given by the architect Luca Beltrami to whom we owe not only the definate salvation of the building, but also his general systematization, the total restoration (the Filarete tower was also reconstructed by Beltrami) and its destination as the home of very important cultural Institutions.

From the end of the last century the Castello Sforzesco occupies once again — with its ornaments of brick and stone, embattlemented barrage, the courtyards, open galleries, moats, towers and large angular, squared or cylindrical towers and friezed by the coats of arms of « large snakes » of the Visconti and the Sforza — a prominent and unmistakable position in the heart of Milan. Inside the large perimeter of the castle, the *Museum of Ancient Art* and the *Pinacotheque,* the *Historical Archives of Milan,* the *Trivulziana Library,* the « *Bertarelli* » *Stamp Collection, the History of Art Library* « *L. Beltrami* » have found worthy and suitable systematization: the portico of the Rocchetta holds a *Lapidary Museum.* In a visit to the castle, every part of it reveals itself to be of great interest, and allows study of the successive phases of the building's development in time: the landscape of the courtyards is exceedingly suggestive (the main one, called « of the Militia », is notable for the presence, among others of some facades of ancient Milanese houses, reconstructed here) and it is also very suggestive in the interiors, the galleries, the communication trenches and on the

tortuous staircase. It is not our job to describe the conspicuous and very rich collections of art which make the Castello Sforzesco one of the most important European museums, in terms of an itinerary or guide: one would, however, say that the *Museum of Ancient Art,* which boasts moreover masterpieces of mediaeval and Renaissance sculpture, is an essential result of the consciousness of the Milanese civilisation, from Roman and Paleo-Christian beginnings onwards, conserving the most fascinating testimonies of such a civilisation — even if sometimes in a transgressional and fragmentary form; one would say also that the *Pinacotheque,* in its numerous rooms, produces the most complete review of Lombardese painting, with frequent and very authoritive exemplification of other Italian and foreign schools of painting (especially the Venetian school). The sequence of collections of « minor » and decorative art works, looked after in the top rooms of the Rocchetta is almost infinite. The best real preparation is yielded by the very delicate studies of museo-graphic systematization, started straight away in the postwar by Costantino Baroni and completed a short time ago.

It is said that the Castello Sforzesco suffered serious damage from aerial bombardments in August 1953: damage which was repaired in the swiftest and most economic way. The City of Milan then indemnified its major Museum in a guise which cannot be imagined as more splendid: reserving one of the highest masterpieces of the art of all time, to be precise, the Rondanini Pietà of Michelangelo for it, acquired in 1952.

29. - UNKNOWN OF THE XV CENTURY

A Story of Griselda. - (Removed fresco) Museum of the Castello Sforzesco.

In around 1460, Pier Maria Rossi, gentleman of Parma, humanist and friend of Lorenzo il Magnifico, had a series of frescoes in a greenish grisaille of chiaroscuro, which illustrated the « Tale of Griselda » by Boccaccio in an extraordinary and fascinating sequence, made in a room of his Castello Roccabianca.

The intention of the elegant gentleman, in the frescoes, was to construct a homage to his beautiful friend, Bianca d'Arluno and at the same time had to demonstrate to her a high gift, love, and fidelity:

they were carried out by a painter who was close in style to Niccolò da Varello, and represent a very brilliant page in international Gothic painting, chivalrous and courteous in the Lombard meaning. The sixteen frescoes divided up on the walls and the four squares on the ceiling of astronomical symbols and astrological representations, were taken off some years ago, and after being part of a private collection, now figure in the Pinacotheque of the Castello Sforzesco, where the original environment has been exceptionally well reconstructed for them.

30. - BONINO DA CAMPIONE

Funeral Monument of Bernabò Visconti. - Castello Sforzesco Museum.

Bonino da Campione carried out, with helpers, the funeral monument of perhaps one of the most celebrated and dreaded Lords of Milan (died 1385), about ten years after having completed his most admired and complex masterpiece, which is the Sepulcre of Cansignorio della Scala at Verona; however proposing again even here « the vaguely fantastic images of an age, not an evokation, which moves », the stiff, bearded and haughty manikin of the knight of little animation in respect of the Scala sculpture type precedents, that also being « impenetrable and inert,

.... rigid and vacant in cold pride ». (P. Toesca). The charger also, not devoid of his latent and primordial power, is constrained in a frozen geometry of lines and volumes which rend it like a huge merry-go-round horse; neither the statuettes and the reliefs of the sarcophagus avail to untie so much archaic rigour, and are proudly raised up from the soil between a good twelve columns and pilasters.

The monument comes from the crypt of the Milanese church of San Giovanni in Conca.

31. - MICHELANGELO BUONARROTI (1475-1564)

Rondanini Pietà. - *Castello Sforzesco Museum.*

In 1952 the Milan Council bought this supreme and very high masterpiece by Michelangelo, which after being left for centuries in the courtyard of the Palazzo Rondanini in Rome, became the property of the Counts Vimercati-Sanseverino: by buying it, the Milanese Council Administration rendered a service of great importance to the city, besides accomplishing a gesture of illuminated Maecenasism.

The stupendous sculpture is the famous last work of the artist who was intent on it right up until a few days before his death, re-elaborating a precedent composition he had been following for round about ten years (and of which we have proof in three drawings at Oxford): some elements of the original version remain in the marble group, like the right arm, strangely detached from the body, the leg of Christ, and some detail of the veil covering the head

of the Virgin; the remainder of the work, with the « unfinished » part, belongs to the last refacing, dramatically interrupted by his death.

« *Death itself* — said Riccardo Bacchelli — *worked to free the artifice from an act of his own willingness, changing in remission. The planes, the roughness, and the masses, concealed by that chisel, render more evident and imperious in this statue .... the relationship and the proportional and harmonic contrasts, the lines and architectural structure, the geometrical figure in which the innumerable rythms of the composition are described, the mystery of a static in which one feels and suffers the inane weight of death, the empty attraction of the tomb, the weight of inert meat, and crush in desparation the force of pain which rises up to love, and rises again in the charity of the mute gesture of the sculptured form* ».

32. - THE ARCHES OF THE PORTA NUOVA

In 1171 rose (without counting the restoration in 1861) the actual form of the twin arched gate, reconstructed in that year; but which previously made part of the circle of walls erected between 1156 and 1158 to defend against Barbarossa (it was the Milanese's authentic « scarecrow » for quite a long time). The two barrel vaults in blocks of black and white marble, today appear rather lost between the enormous modern buildings which seem to overwhelm it and it seems only to have a value as a symbol — but what a symbol! — the proud resistence of the Milan Council against the most furious and overbearing aggressors, the Emperor of Germany and against its few non-exemplary allied Italians.

Much of the history of Milan has been found in the subsoil during recent excavations, when important architectural remains came to light there, while on the inside fronts of the arches fitted in Roman fragments appear. The outside front, instead, figures a marble tabernacle with the *Madonna and Son, and the Saints Ambrose, Gervase and Protasio,* referable to around the first forty years of the XIV century, and probably a work of a student of Giovanni di Balduccio.

33. - THE COLUMNS OF SAN LORENZO

To look at them, these sixteen isolated columns lined up in an abstract space, they seem as though someone has gone to the trouble to strip them in some places, as we used to with the trunks of trees sometimes: but instead no, it has been time alone. These high, grooved columns, ornamented by elegant Corinthian capitals, in antiquity made part of a not very good classical Roman building of the decline (II-III centuries, someone has mentioned, from the palace of the Emperor Massimiano Eruleo), and today they are the most conspicuous testimony of the Roman *Mediolanum*. They were brought here and placed all in a line in the IV century to make the principal front to the quadriportico of the Basilica of San Lorenzo, which was then being constructed.

The singular monument has the quality, no less singular, of rising up in a place most significative and rich in suggestions in Milan: in fact, behind it is the majestic Basilica of San Lorenzo, a prominent example of Paleo-Christian architecture, although we see it today in the dress of the sixth century, carried out by Martino Bassi, keeping to the original plan and proportions; a short time before this, the very original and turreted Porta Ticinese was built, communal and for the viscountcy, proud passageway, obligatory from long tradition of every famous personage who arrives in the city; lastly, the same road, colourful and picturesque, is still today one of those that best show the character, between poetic and modest, of old Milan.

34 - 35. · THE PARK AND THE ARCH OF PEACE

From mediaeval to neoclassical, from a forest of the princes to a public garden: this is the secular metamorphasis of, exactly, the Park, that place of rural and wooded charm, rich with shadowy suggestions of light and tone (of the spring, autumn and winter), that very romantic oasis destined to make every preconceived common place fall regarding an unromantic or antiromantic Milan. This same Park finally, is no other but a part of the antique and immense park of the Sforza family, reduced to its actual design by the architect Alemagna in 1893. Very dear to Milanese of all ages and conditions, it takes into its perimeter the *Palazzo dell'Arte,* aulic seat of the « Triennale of Decorative Art », the little (but not so little) Milanese « Eiffel » which is the *Torre del Parco* (109,95 m.) and the old and glorious *Arena* (by Luigi Canonica, 1805-1806), fore-

runner of all Italian sporting establishments, and which had the rare priviledge to be inaugurated by Napoleon with nothing less than a chariot race.

Indeed a certain Napoleonic, Imperial, Parisian air circulates — looking carefully — around these parts, starting from the scenographic perspective which stretches from the Castello, crossing the whole park (and let us however put to one side the equestrian monument of Napoleon III), as far as the large « Etoile » which is formed around the *Arch of Peace* by Luigi Cagnoli, started in 1807 and finished, see how strange, in the full climate of Hapsburg restoration in 1838; complete with a « sestiga » (for the chronicles, a six horse chariot), winged victories and allegorical bass reliefs etc. In 1859, Victor Emanuele II and Napoleon II, Emperor of the French, passed under it in triumph.

36. - SANTA MARIA DELLE GRAZIE

The Church of Santa Maria delle Grazie is one of the great monuments — perhaps the most influentual — of Lombardian Renaissance, in the sphere of those happy relations matured between Milan and Central Italy towards the end of the fifteenth century and centred around the names of Leonardo and Bramante: a famous example of Tuscan architectural forms inserted over a pre-existing structure of late Gothic taste, with full comprehension and acception on the part of the last architect, however (in our case, to be exact, Bramante) of the colouristic and decorative requirements of the Lombard atmosphere.

On the spot where Santa Maria delle Grazie stands, previously, in antique times, there was a chapel with frescoes with images of the *Madonna of Grace*: the ground was given to the Domenicans in 1463, by the Count Gaspare Vimercati, Captain of the Militia of Francesco Sforza; and the brothers commissioned the architect Guineforte Solari to construct the convent and church there. The convent was finished already by 1469; the church was, instead, built between 1466 and '90, and Solari conceived it, so it is said, in terms still adherent to the Gothic tradition, with an ample facade of the Lombard style (the doorway that one sees there was in fact added by Bramante) and the interior, of three naves with ogive arches, cross vaults and chapels that opened off along the minor naves. The intact suggestions of this interior, composed and measured in a balanced equilibrium of form, is still worthy today, confirming how the Lombardese architect, advanced already for the fifteenth century, could use the force of Gothic suggestions.

Solario had completed the church with the presbytery and apse; but here, the humanistic ambition of Ludovico il Moro prevailed towards the end of the century, and he decreed, notwithstanding the fact that the church was only just finished, that it was to have a new, more ample and representative conclusion and, had the presbytery and apse demolished, and called in Bramante to replace them with a grandiose tribune of higher tone and very different proportions and forms. Bramante started the work in March 1492, and in 1497, Ludovico il Moro was able to bury, in the new monument of his desire, Beatrice d'Este, his deceased wife.

The Bramantesque assumption, in obedience to the prince's wish, was really grandiose in its spacial concept as in its proportions: the massive tribune, on a squared plan, supported by three apses, was raised up mightily and, at the same time, very elegantly, surmounted by the high polygonal tiburium. The complaint of the fundamental idea as being a lesson of Brunelleschi (that actuated above all in the Pazzi Chapel and in the Sacresty of San Lorenzo in Florence), is however in the fullness of the renewed and luminous vision, an evident result, especially in the inside of the « cube » of the tribune. There, on the frames where the arches are placed destined to join the inferior space, cubic exactly, with that of the hemisphere of the dome; the great tondoes in the pendentive reappear, and the plan of the « umbrella » dome is reposed (that which Brunelleschi would have derived from the Byzantine dome of Constantinople). But the space, however in its distinct rigour appears much more moved and fragmented by the insistence and the picturesqueness of the decoration; by the surprising repetition *ad infinitum,* of the motif of the circle, of the windows, the tondoes of the frames, and the superb turn of the radiant wheels on the triumphal arch: splendid symbol of the conquered perfection.

The thing that hits one most in the interior of this church, is the contrast between the neat Gothic elegance of the naves and the coloured and very reasoned space of the tribune: a convincing example however of noble « co-existence » of form and concepts, clearly antitetical, between them. The exterior of the tribune and the apse show that Bramante principally if induced, in the rest, to concede to the taste and to the tradition of Lombardy, collects precious advice also; the moved and very articulate covering of the apse is revealed as the most qualified to pick up the subtle and precious play of the brickwork, displayed in the tondoes, frames, the moulding, in the motifs of amprorae, and in the refined candelabra.

The very beautiful Sacresty is also owed to Donato Bramante, rich with stupendous wooden marquetry, and the elegant little Cloister; « the Large Cloister », the work, instead, of Solari, and destroyed by the bombing of 1943, has been reconstructed in a dissimilar way to the original.

37. - LEONARDO DA VINCI (1452-1519)

Last Supper. - (Fresco) Santa Maria delle Grazie; Cenacolo

Few works in the world are more famous and « popular » than the Last Supper frescoed by Leonardo in the Cenacolo of Santa Maria delle Grazie in Milan. More, we would like to say, than the same high quality of the painting, it is thanks to the very copious literary and anecdotical incrustations, and in virtue of the abnormal vicissitudes of the unfortunate painting, also.

The work had a somewhat discontinued genesis, if we must believe Bandello, eye witness « *in the time of Ludovico Sforza Visconte, Duke of Milan* »; he narrates that Leonardo, « *used not to put down his brush from the dawning sun to darkening evening, but used to forget food and drink by continually painting* » meanwhile « *two, three even four days sometimes passed and he did not touch his brushes* »; and yet another time the painter would « *take the brush and give one or two strokes to one of the figures and leave at once to go elsewhere* ». The famous da Vinci « supper piece » was carried out between 1495 and 1497, with a completely unusual

and unfortunately deceptive technique, to a point that its degradation was immediate and very rapid (so that Vasari, just seventy years afterwards, was only able to discern a « bewildering light »). There were many endeavours at restoration from 1726 to 1928; but it is not said that they have not contributed to make the situation worse in many ways: the last conservative restoration is of recent years, after the fresco was miraculously saved in the bombing of '43, which destroyed almost all of the refectory.

In spite of the very grave, unarrestable deterioration which has reduced it to a little less than phantasmal state, the Last Supper of Leonardo keeps its charm of very high invention intact, which it gave off before, and confirms, in the very clever space, in the magic vicissitudes of light, in the human and spiritual fullness of the emotive and however controlled personages, the pictorical genius of the artist of whom one can say — as Berenson has already in 1896 — that « nothing he touched was not transformed into eternal beauty ».

38. - THE LAZZARETTO

« *Imagine, reader, the enclosure of the Lazzaretto, left crowded with the languishing, the space all cluttered up here with huts and barracks, and there with carts and persons; those two unfinished files of porticoes, full to the right and the left, crowded with the languishing, the confused corpses on straw mattresses or on the straw itself; and above all, that almost huge wretched abode swarming like waves; and here and there a coming and going, or a stopping, and a running or a bending, a raising of convalescents, ravers and of orderlies* ». (A. Manzoni, *I Promessi Sposi,* Chapter XXXV).

Thanks to Manzoni, the plague in 1630 (on which he wrote very learnedly the Ripamonte in five volumes, « *cronista urbis Mediolani* », in 1640) became the most famous plague of all time, the plague for antonomasia; and it was that which horribly decreased the population of Milan, and not only Milan. The very little that has been preserved of the Lazzaretto remains today the only visible testimony of such a very wretched event: a short feature along the road which is now Via San Gregorio, on the northwest side of the immense quadrilateral portico (m. 370 × 378) which surrounded this Lazzaretto, exactly: such a fragment still conserves at the inside edges, some arches of the portico under which opened off the isolation wards, each one with a window over the road. The Lazzaretto, started by Lazzaro (see how strange!) Palazzi in 1488 was finished in 1629: as wished by San Carlo Borromeo, an octagonal church stood in the centre (today *San Carlo al Lazzaretto* by Pellegrini) originally open on both sides to allow the hospital occupants to follow the carrying on of the rites from the outside.

39. - THE BASIN OF THE PORTA TICINESE

There is no doubt: the biggest stroke against the traditional and « romantic » face of Milan was made by the filling in and therefore the disappearance of the circle of the Naviglio canal, a pathetic road of water not avaricious of silences, of dangling greenery, of gardens fronted by balustrades: twilight itinerary of poets.

When Via Senato was Via Senato,
and the Naviglio was still alive,
roses flowered in the gardens.

(L. Broggini).

Urbane reasons, the necessity of traffic; but all the same it was a great pity. Only one reminder is left: however one needs to go and look a little further afield, between the Porta Genova and the Porta Ticinese, where the rectilineal Grand Naviglio and the Pavia Naviglio converge. But the Basin is anyway thick with cement, surrounded by big houses all alike (they say that they want to cover even that), and always graver, make themselves the impending menaces on the « hawsers » and the « banks », last unreal landscapes, half Venice and half Holland, of Milan. Meanwhile, the big green carriages of the trams which rattle along the narrow shore make an effect of running on a Venetian foundation.

SANT'EUSTORGIO

40. - THE BELL-TOWER AND THE PORTINARI CHAPEL
41. - GIOVANNI DI BALDUCCIO: *The Tomb of St. Peter Martyr*

A facade, in itself complex, modest and we would like to say, impressive enough (by force, it is a refacing of 1863!), on a little tree covered square, the few rapid and light shadows on the pebbles: on the other side of the road, the Corsa di Porta Ticinese, old, low houses (who knows for how long they have been here), shop signs are skilfully pulled out. A facade which does not make one hope for much, it is said; but to heighten the prestige, on the left, in the corner, there is a small aedicula of 1597, erected to the memory of St. Peter of Verona, martyr of the religion, and basis of the Order of the Preaching Friars. In the centre of the square, on the top of a high column stands a statue of St. Peter the Martyr. Without doubt, the righthand side is more interesting, a long file of aristocratic chapels of the XIV and XV centuries (of the Brivio, Torelli, Crotti, Visconti, Torriani families): then the powerful apse, of which remains some of the primative construction of the IX century, and the high and uplifting Lombardian belfry; finally the precious addition of the Portinari Chapel.

The interior of the church (better to say the Basilica), brings us foward to a climax of extraordinary and almost unexpected mystic suggestions: that spacious vault, in the faint light of the central nave; the unheard of force of the cruciform pilasters which support it, or those cylindrical, thickset, low and misteriously ponderous ones. Here and there are fragments of archaic votive frescoes of the XIII and XIV centuries.

A little of the history. The Basilica of Sant'Eustorgio, numbering among the most illustrious Romanic monuments of Milan, was erected towards the end of the IX century, and was also in correspondence with a Paleo-Christian cemetary (the remains are visible today in the basement), and on the site of a very antique church of the IV century, of the time of Bishop Eustorgio I. All of it, save the apse, was renovated in the XII century; in 1290 the Domenicans replaced the trussed vaults of the ceiling, and from 1297 to 1309 constructed the belfry. Almost useless to join that, between the XVI and XVIII centuries, the church underwent disfiguring alterations, to which were added praiseworthy repairs in the course of restoration started in 1862.

It is the case to say also that one of the major merits of this church is that which comes to it from the extraordinary quantity and quality of sculpture which are collected in it (a real museum!): to start with, the Funeral Monument of *Giacomo Stefano Brivio* (died 1484), that of *Tommaso Cazzaniga,* then following them, that of *Pietro Torelli* (died 1416), the work of Jacopino da Tradate, with the grandiose *Mausoleum of Stefano Visconti* (died 1327) and his wife, attributed in part to Giovanni di Balduccio and finished by Bonino da Campione; then, again, the Tomb of Gaspare Visconti, that of Umberto Visconti, the tomb slab of Agnese Besozzi, attributed to Jacopino da Tradate, the fourteenth century sarcophagus of Protaso Caimo, and the sepulcre of the Bishop Federico de' Maggi (died 1333).

Other motifs of conspicuous interest are offered in Sant'Eustorgio by the remains of the primative apse brought to light in the artificial crypt, and the immense Roman sarcophagus, touching for its clear significance, for in it would have been preserved the bodies of the Magi, the three kings, Caspar, Melchior and Balthassar until 1164, given in consignment by Emperor Constantine to Milan. Neither does the head of St. Peter the Martyr with its terrifying wound caused by the heretics' knife, miss producing a certain effect, solitary and lost in its silver and crystal case in the centre of a little chapel.

THE PORTINARI CHAPEL

This is not only the most illustrious monument among all those included in the limits of Sant'Eustorgio, but also one of the most authorative testimonies of the early Renaissance in Milan. It was started by a commission given in 1462 by Pigello Portinari, agent of the Medici Bank in Milan; at the death of the purchaser in 1468, the chapel was already ready to have his mortal remains placed inside. The attribution, unsupported by documents, to the Florentine Michelozzo di Bartolomeo is variously received by critics: there rests the fact, in any case, that the

Portinari Chapel represents one of the first transpositions in Lombardian key on Brunelleschian themes (one notes the colouristic novelty introduced by the use of bricks in the frame); and also the monument therefore constitutes a steady point in the history of Milanese architecture, anticipating in a certain sense, the coming Bramante expreriences. The walls are adorned with frescoes of the *Annunciation,* the *Assumption,* and the *History of St. Peter the Martyr,* masterpiece of Vincenzo Foppa (1465): up aloft are Angels, Apostles and Doctors of the Church,

and everywhere a profusion of exquisite reliefs and coloured stuccoes: however it is clear that it deals with a type of architecture with too many relevant signs of Tuscan origins, although in the pompous Lombard meaning.

In the centre is the *Tomb of St. Peter Martyr,* masterpiece of 14th century Milanese sculpture by Giovanni di Balduccio who carved it between 1336 and 1339. This Pisan sculptor worked in Lombardy for a long time, always obtaining success.

MODERN MILAN

42. - MILAN « LA NUIT »
43. - THE SKYSCRAPERS
44. - THE MILAN FAIR
45. - THE « METRÒ »

The Milanese must not think, all so justly proud of the « modernity » and « modernism » of their city, that we would have wanted in some way to mortify — exalting up until now, the monumental and artistic Milan and the « romantic » Milan above all — this given essential and finally, today, constitutional Milan itself. They calm themselves by saying that is not entirely like this. On the other hand, it is not possible anymore — even if one wished to — to separate the modern Milan today from the old one, or simply the oldest: because anyway, the modern is infiltrated almost everywhere it has been left, seems as though it is contaminated, « made dynamic » by the modernity that tugs at the city.

One would say then that the modernity of Milan does not have the inhuman and frozen aspect that it could have, instead elsewhere: it has assumed on the contrary rather an affable domestic air (the crystal palaces that sparkle fabulously at night, they seem equally as though they are enchanted castles; and it is not true in the least, at the bottom, that the skyscrapers give all that annoyance, that one could believe, to the spires of the Duomo and to the Madonnina). The skyscrapers already are one of the many motives for pride on the part of the Milanese of today; there are, anyway, a great many, of which some are masterpieces of the technician and of architecture of our times. Do we want to re-

remember two or three of the most important? Here: the Pirelli skyscraper, m. 127, the « skyscraper of Milan », m. 114, in Via Vittor Pisani, and the Torre Velasca: then, the others that have risen already in more points of the city, characterising its profile and making it like a little and rarified « Manhattan ».

By modern today, naturally, many things are intended: progress, commodity, facility of communication, an amplitude of « infrastructure », social and cultural equipment, amusements, playing fields, development of technological and scientific research, etc. There is no doubt that here, with all this, Milan has no fear of rivals, at least in Italy: this Milan which does not lack seaplane stations, swimming pools, palaces and sports arenas, ice rinks, cycle racing tracks, hippodromes, arenas and stadiums, conscience of the proper destiny of the city irremediably « of the plain », and picked by perhaps an unexpected (but probably already atavistic) desire to ascend, there have been constructed, besides those skyscrapers already mentioned, an artificial hill, the « Q.T.8 » (not higher, it is true, than about fifty metres: however...).

Even in this article there will not be missed out a due hint of the Milanese industries, those which really make Milan, without any rhetoric, « the pulsing heart of the nation ». And here in the main part because (however leaving out the great sweet-making

industries like Motta and Alemagna) the principal Milanese industries (Montecatini-Edison, Pirelli, Snia-Viscosa, Falk, Marelli Group) give work to around 57.000 dependents in Milan alone, and outside Milan, in the rest of Italy, to another 178.000. Neither can

one leave out finally, the great *Trade Fair,* one of the greatest in Europe and the world, an influention international emporium of commerce and traffic, and which displays every year its shining *kermess* over a surface of its expositional seat, the pavilions included that have the most floors and pavilions in the open, the road and squares of 638.771 square metres, which the ground area alone is of 400.000 square metres.

How many inhabitants can Milan count today in its municipal territory? In October 1967 there were exactly one million, 683.328: a respectable figure, and it is enlarged in grandiose terms if one keeps count of the population of the very vast *banlieu* and of the « commutor's trains ». To make the internal shifting of so many considerable portions of humanity, easier, and to give at the same time, a final touch to the preparation of a metropolis that Milan has all the right to concede to itself, here is what in the last few years the Council has done to give a hand to construct a metropolitan railway, obviously the most modern and the most elegant in Europe. The first line, inaugurated towards the end of 1964 (in the direction of Sesto-Marelli and Lotto-Gambara), measures 14,700 Km. The second line in construction (partly underground, partly above), will have a total development of 26,600 Km. The Milanese call this their Metropolitan (on the example of the most famous one in the world, the one in Paris; and moving only the placing of the accent) the *metrò*.

INDEX

ARTISTIC ITALY

is a series of publications illustrating the masterpieces of art in Museums, Churches and Palaces throughout Italy.
A new guide to the most significant works of the old masters. A guide for visiting the places where are to be found the masterpieces of all time which today form the artistic wealth of Italy.

OF THIS SERIES THE FOLLOWING HAVE ALREADY BEEN PUBLISHED:

THE PIAZZA OF MIRACLES *by Riccardo Barsotti*

STROLLING THROUGH VERONA *by Renzo Chiarelli*

MICHELANGELO IN FLORENCE *by Nils Martellucci*

MICHELANGELO IN ROME *by Nils Martellucci*

THE UFFIZI GALLERY *by M. Lenzini - E. Micheletti*

THE PITTI PALACE *by Emma Micheletti*

GET TO KNOW MILAN *by Renzo Chiarelli*

ALL ROME AND THE VATICAN *by Eugenio Pucci*

THE ACADEMY GALLERY

AND THE MUSEUM OF ST. MARK *by Renzo Chiarelli*

FIRENZE *by Edoardo Bonechi*

Direttore Responsabile VITTORIO CUMINETTI
Condirettore   GIAMPAOLO BONECHI

Segreteria di Redazione - LIA MONTANARI
Stampa - ARTI GRAFICHE PARIGI E MAGGIORELLI - Firenze
Fotolito - LA FOTOLITOGRAFIA - Firenze
Servizio Fotografico eseguito da GAETANO BARONE

Autorizzazione del Tribunale di Firenze n. 1835 del 31-5-67
Spedizione a tariffa editoriale ridotta

Lire 1.000

DATE DUE

APR 18		
APR 30		
DEC 15		

The Library Store   #47-0103